CW01512573

THIS JOURNAL BELONGS To

....

"Self-reflection is the
school of wisdom."

– Balthasar Gracián

GOODBYE
2025
HELLO

As one year comes to an end and another begins, it's time to take a step back, to pause for a moment in the rush of life and reflect on the year you've just lived through and the year that lies ahead.

To recognise and acknowledge all that has happened, all that you've done and all that you're grateful for having experienced: the lessons, the love, the achievements, the people and the moments that marked this year and made it unique.

And then it's time to close the chapter on 2025, turn your focus to the year that lies ahead and let yourself dream. Ask yourself what you really want, how you want to feel and which of your dreams you want to dedicate yourself to bringing to life this coming year.

So let's do that.

Let's say a proper farewell to 2025 and get ready to create the life you want to live in 2026.

HOW To USE THIS JOURNAL

Goodbye 2025, Hello 2026 is a reflective end-of-year journal that, through a series of questions and exercises, helps you to say a proper farewell to 2025 as it comes to an end and create a vision and a plan for the year to come.

The journal then becomes your guide to designing a life you love in 2026 with quarterly check-ins throughout the year to keep you on track as you go after your dreams and goals.

But while this is a guided journal, it's still your journal. There is no wrong or right way to fill it in. Write, draw, scribble in the margins. The most important thing is that you do it in a way that feels good to you.

You might do it in one sitting or you might do it in a series of mini-sessions. You might do it on solo dates with yourself or you might do it with friends, as a way of sharing your dreams with one another.

Write as little or as much as you like (there are blank pages in the back if you need more space). If you find yourself drawing a blank with any of the questions, you can always leave it and come back to it later or skip it all together. Not every question will feel relevant to you this year.

Above all, have fun with it and enjoy seeing what answers emerge on the page.

I can't wait to see what it does for you!

X Selina
Creator of this journal :)

JOIN THE GODBYE HELLO CLUB!

Join the Goodbye Hello Club (it's free!) and get bonus exercises, reminders when it is time to do your quarterly check-in and invitations to join live online journaling sessions where you can fill in your journal with me and **Goodbye, Hello** fans all over the world!

Join the club today by scanning the QR code here or going to projectyoujournals.com/ goodbye-hello-club

"We do not learn from experience...
we learn from reflecting on experience."

– John Dewey

BYE 2025

"You have to look back in order to understand the things that lie ahead."

– Yvonne Woon

WHAT HAPPEN IN 2025

A lot can change and a lot can happen in just one year. So, now it's time to take a step back and reflect on what happened in your life in 2025.

Those twelve months will have been filled with happiness, sadness, celebrations and challenges. And throughout it all you will have learned valuable lessons that will have helped you to grow.

So, now on the following pages you'll be answering questions designed to help you reflect on all that happened in your life in 2025, from the milestones, to your happiest moments, to your hardest moments and everything in between.

If at first you find it hard to recall things, take it slowly. Go month by month, perhaps using your calendar or photos you have taken to help remind you of what you did over the past year.

Remember that there are no right or wrong answers to any of these questions. You might have just a few lines to write for one question, but with others, you might have so much you want to write that you'll need to use the extra pages at the back of the book.

The key to answering these questions is to relax, spend a little time pondering each question and enjoy this process of reflecting and spending quality time with yourself.

A LOT CAN CHANGE, A LOT CAN HAPPEN IN JUST ONE YEAR.

LET'S SEE WHAT'S HAPPENED IN YOUR LIFE...

What was going on in your life this time last year?

How were you feeling?

As you looked ahead to 2025, what did you want it to be all about for you?

What were the main events and milestones in your life in 2025?

What did you create, achieve and make happen in 2025?
(the big and the small)

What were your happiest moments?

When did you have the most fun?

When and where did you feel the most at peace?

What has been the most unexpected thing about this year?

What new thing(s) did you discover about yourself?

When did you feel the most love?

What have been your hardest moments?

What have been your biggest challenges?

What are you particularly proud of yourself for?

What are the most important lessons you have learned?

What will 2025 be remembered for in your life?

"Wear gratitude like a cloak and it will feed every corner of your life."

– Yvonne Woon

TUDE

THE POWER OF GRATITUDE

Gratitude is the simple but powerful practice of expressing thanks and giving appreciation for what you have in your life, right now.

Practicing gratitude for what you already have is a key tool when it comes to designing a life you love because when you ground yourself in gratitude, you cultivate a positive mindset. You come from a place of abundance and thanks, rather than a place of lack and scarcity.

You are far more likely to believe in your dreams and go towards the things that bring you joy and happiness.

So let's get you grounding yourself in gratitude, by reflecting on the things that you are grateful for **right now** in your life.

What are you grateful for in your life at the moment?

Who are you grateful for?

What about yourself are you grateful for this year?

"The things that excite you are not random. They are connected to your purpose. Follow them."

– Fabienne Fredrickson

YOU

WHAT
MAKES
YOU FEEL
HAPPY,
ALIVE AND
FULFILLED
IN LIFE?

WHAT DO YOU WANT To FILL YOUR LiFe WiTH?

Now that you've said a proper farewell to 2025, it's time to turn your attention towards 2026. A fresh new canvas lies ahead of you. So what do you want to fill those days with?

In order for you to be able to answer that, you first need to be clear on what it is you need in life **right now** to feel truly happy, alive, at peace and fulfilled.

And that is what this next section is all about.

Over the following pages, you're going to build up a juicy list of all the things that make you happy in life: the activities that make you come alive, the people that bring you joy and the places you love to spend time in.

You're going to look back to some of your happiest times in life and the ingredients that helped make you so happy and then you're going to allow yourself to imagine what you would love your dream life to look like five years from now.

As in the previous section, there are no right or wrong answers to any of these questions. You might have lots to write for one and just a sentence to write on the next. And don't be surprised if you find yourself repeating some answers – this just helps to highlight what is particularly important to you at the moment.

Relax your mind, let your imagination go and see what emerges on the page in front of you as you start to write...

WHAT ARE THE
THINGS YOU LOVE TO DO?

What simple pleasures do you enjoy?

What activities make you come alive?

What activities help you to feel calm and relaxed?

What do you love to do on your time off or at the weekend?

What do you love to do on holiday?

What are things you've tried once or did a long time ago, that you'd love to do again?

What activities do you love to do with the people you love?

What activities do you love to do on your own?

Think back to your happiest moments in life – what were you doing that made you so happy?

WHERE ARE THE PLACES YOU LOVE TO BE?

Where do you feel your happiest? (This can be a specific place, such as at home, or a more general area, for example, by the sea)

What places (or kinds of places) do you feel most at peace and relaxed in?

Where are the places that you have the most fun?

What are the kinds of places you like to visit on holiday?

What places in the world would you one day love to visit?

Think back to your happiest moments in life – where were you that made you so happy?

WHO ARE THE PEOPLE
YOU LOVE TO BE WITH?

Who are the people you love to spend time with? And why?

Who are the people that inspire you? And why? (You can include people you know, people you follow online or even fictional or historical characters.)

Who do you feel most supported by when it comes to creating a life you love?

Who do you want to support in creating a life that they love?

Who would you love to spend more time with in 2026?

WHAT MAKES YOU FEEL GOOD IN YOUR BODY?

What helps you to feel good in your body and mind?
(E.g. plenty of water, exercise, eight hours of sleep, yoga, meditation etc...)

What helps to recharge your batteries when you've tired yourself out?

HOW DO YOU LIKE TO FEEL?

When you're at your happiest at home, how do you feel?

When you're at your happiest at work, how do you feel?

When you're at your happiest on your own, how do you feel?

WHAT LIFE DO YOU DREAM OF?

YOU ARE NEVER TOO OLD TO SET ANOTHER GOAL OR TO DREAM A NEW DREAM.

– C.S.Lewis

TAKE YOUR DREAMS SERIOUSLY

Our ability to dream things up and then make those dreams happen is the very real magic we have as human beings. It is what gives us the power to be able to bring about change in our own lives and in the world around us.

But as we grow up, we are often told to stop dreaming and start getting serious about life. But what if, instead, we are meant to get serious about our dreams and use the power we have to turn those dreams into reality?
The next section of this journal invites you to do just that.

Over the following pages you're invited to dream and to dream BIG. Let yourself imagine that anything is possible and see what dreams emerge when you allow yourself to do that.

YOUR DREAM LIFE

The key to dreaming and dreaming big is to give yourself permission –
permission to imagine that anything is possible and to dream from there.

So let's imagine you have a magic wand that you can use to conjure
up whatever you want in your own life: your dream home, dream career,
dream relationship – whatever it is you want, you can have it.

Now imagine that you're living that life five years from now.

Take yourself there for a moment and describe what that life is like. And
don't hold back. Let yourself dream as wildly as your imagination allows...

Where do you live?

What is your home like?

How do you spend your days?

What do you do on your time off?

What kind of holidays do you go on?

Who are the special people in your life?

What have you achieved over the past five years? (Remember that this is five years into the future.)

Is there anything else you can see in this dream life of yours?

How does it feel to live this life?

What is it that you love the MOST about this life of yours?

YOU ARE NEVER GIVEN A DREAM WITHOUT ALSO BEING GIVEN THE POWER TO MAKE IT TRUE.

– Richard Bach

As you look at your 'dream life', what aspects of it would you most like to start bringing to life in 2026?

What practical steps can you take to get started on bringing those dreams to life in 2026?

"Now is the time to start living
the life you've imagined."
– Henry James

2026

LIVING A LIFE YOU LOVE IN 2026

A fresh new year lies ahead of you. A blank canvas for you to paint with the things you love. A whole new chapter in your life for you to write.

So... what do you want to fill your life with in 2026? What do you want it to be all about?

It's time to choose.

As you look back at your answers in this journal so far, it's time to see which dreams are calling to you the most, which ingredients you most want to fill this year with and what intention you want to set for yourself and your life in 2026.

Over the following pages, you'll be asked questions designed to help you get clear on what you want to make your 2026 all about.

Don't worry if you don't have an answer to every question. Just answer the ones that speak to you. As with every other section, you will likely find that there are some questions you have clear answers for, while others don't feel so relevant to you this year.

So grab your pen and get ready to decide what life you want to design for yourself in 2026.

WHAT DO YOU WANT To
MAKE YOUR 2026 ALL ABOUT?

What do you want your life to be full of in 2026? (write down your favourite ingredients from your answers in the Hello You section and anything else you think of)

Which of your dreams do you want to bring to life (or start to bring to life) this year?

What challenges or projects do you want to take on this year?

What positive changes do you want to make to your life this year?

What do you want less of in your life in 2026?

What do you want more of in your life in 2026?

What self-care practices do you want to maintain or add into your daily or weekly life in 2026 to help you to thrive?

Read through each of the feelings
on these pages and circle the ones
that call to you the most.

CALM - JOYFUL - AT PEACE
- HAPPY - INSPIRED -
AT EaSE - CONNECTED
- FoCUSED - PLAYFUL -
IN MY POWER - CONTENT
- FULFiLLED - ABUNDANT -
ALiVE - NOURISHED
- FrEE - SERENE - BOLD -
GRatEFUL - COURAGEoUS
- EXPANSIVE - TRuSTiNG -
VIBRANT - UNSToPPABLE
- ROOTED - CONFiDENT -
BLiSSFUL - AUTHENTIC
- MOTiVaTED - RADIANT -

- PASSIONATE - RELAXED - EMPOWERED - SENSUAL - RESTED - GROUNDED - LIGHT - BALANCED - BOLD - FULL OF LOVE - TENDER - OPTIMISTIC - IN FLOW - PRESENT - ENERGISED - FILLED UP - HOPEFUL - POSITIVE - UPLIFTED -

Now choose one to three feelings that you most want to experience in 2026, adding any of your own if you don't see them here.

In 2026 I want to feel...

"What you think, you become.
What you feel, you attract.
What you imagine, you create."

– Buddha

SETTING INTENT!

OK, now we are getting to the big moment in your Goodbye, Hello journey: it's time for you to choose your focus for the new year.

What do you want to make 2026 all about? What do you want your focus to be?

Setting an intention for your year acts like a gentle but powerful anchor, keeping you focused on what is most important to you, reminding you of what it is you want more of in your life and helping you stay committed to the dreams and projects that have you creating the life you want to live.

Setting an intention also has a certain magic to it that setting a specific goal doesn't. When you set an intention you don't always know how it is going to take shape in your life. Sometimes it will occur in ways that you never imagined. Watching the seed of your intention take root and grow in your life, sometimes in unexpected ways, is all part of the magic and power of intention setting.

Over the following pages, you'll find guidance on how to choose your intention. Ultimately it is about choosing a focus for the year that makes you feel good when you imagine a whole year of making that a priority.

So, turn the page and let's get you setting an intention you love in 2026.

YOUR
N

HOW TO SET A POWERFUL INTENTION FOR YOUR YEAR

The intention you set for 2026 will help to inspire and guide you throughout the year. So the idea is to choose something that inspires you, that feels good and that helps you to design a life you love in the year to come.

Here are some different ways to choose the intention you want to set for 2026:

Option 1:
Set an intention around how you want to feel in 2026

You might be longing to feel a certain way: calm, content, at peace, grounded, joyful, playful, inspired, connected, full of love...

And so you could make that your focus for 2026 and commit to doing the things that help you to feel that way on a regular basis:

'2026 is my year of calm'
'2026 is my year of joy'
'2026 is my year of love'

Option 2:
Set an intention around something you want your life to be full of in 2026

Creativity, fun, adventure, celebration, nourishment, laughter, clarity, gratitude, self-care, connection, vitality, self-love:

'2026 is my year of fun'
'2026 is my year of creativity'
'2026 is my year of self-care'

Option 3:
Set an intention around a big dream or a big change you want to make in your life

If this is the year you really feel ready to commit and make that big change happen, or bring that big dream to life, then setting it as your intention for the year can really help to fire up your commitment and make it your central focus:

'2026 is my year of starting my own business'
'2026 is my year of finding an exciting new career path'
'2026 is my year of buying my first home'
'2026 is my year of creating my home in a new country'
'2026 is my year of taking a six-month sabbatical'

That said, even if you do have a big change you want to make or a big dream you want to bring to life in 2026, you don't have to choose that as your focus. You might prefer to focus on how you want to approach making that change. For example, you might want 2026 to be the year that you really get your career change going, but rather than making 2026 your year of 'career change', you might choose to make it your year of 'self-care', to help you focus on looking after your wellbeing while you go through a big life change.

Option 4:
Set an intention around growth, healing or transformation
Maybe this year you feel called to grow in a certain way, to heal or to embrace life in a new and empowering way

If so, that could be the focus for your intention:

'2026 is my year of stepping into my power'
'2026 is my year of standing in love'
'2026 is my year of healing'
'2026 is my year of saying "yes!"'

Option 5:
Just go with what your gut says

If you just know what you want your focus for 2026 to be, even if it doesn't fit into Options 1 to 4, then go for it. The key with setting an intention for the year is that it is meaningful and inspiring to you.

NOW IT'S TIME FOR YOU TO SET YOUR INTENTION FOR 2026...

2026 IS
MY YEAR OF

....

YOU'VE SET YOUR INTENTION FOR 2026 – NOW LET'S BRING IT TO LIFE

Why do you want 2026 to be your year of

....?

What are you going to do to make it about that?

NOW LET'S MAKE IT HAPPEN...

"Design a life you are inspired to live."

– Annette White

DESIG
YOUR

NING
LIFE

HOW To DESIGN A LIFE YOU LOVE

Designing a life you love doesn't happen by accident. Whatever your dreams, desires, and visions for this year and the future are, it isn't luck that will make them happen. It is you committing to those dreams and turning them into projects and actionable steps that will ultimately turn your dreams into reality.

And so, in this next part of the journal that's what you're going to be focused on doing, using simple, but powerful life design tools and practices that have been helping people turn their dreams into reality for decades...

Let's go!

YOUR LIFE
DESIGN PLAN

YOUR YEARLY LIFE DESIGN PLAN

You are the artist of your own life and your calendar is the canvas that you get to paint on and fill with the ingredients you want your life to be filled with.

So to start painting your canvas, let's look at 2026 as a whole year. What ingredients do you want to fill this year with?

Are there any trips you want to go on, any birthdays or anniversaries you want to celebrate, any courses you want to do or challenges you want to take on?

Start to plot them out in your yearly life design planner on the following page.

You might also like to set intentions for certain months or seasons. I like to make January the warm up month of the year and mark the whole month as 'Slowanuary' and then I like to do the same in the summer and name July and August as my 'Slow down Summer'.

You might like to pencil things in at first, particularly if you are plotting out big commitments that you aren't yet 100% sure about, but want to explore further. Plot them out for now in pencil.

For now add one or two key commitments or desires into your calendar. Things that you are excited about and you can keep coming back to this yearly planner as you make more plans for your year.

2026

JANUARY

FEBRUARY

MARCH

APRIL

MAY

JUNE

JULY

AUGUST

SEPTEMBER

OCTOBER

NOVEMBER

DECEMBER

YOUR QUARTERLY LIFE DESIGN PLAN

The secret to designing a life you love is to keep it simple and break things down into manageable chunks. So, instead of trying to tackle an entire year all at once, we're going to divide it up into manageable three-month chapters, so that you'll be designing a life you love, one quarter at a time, using your 'Quarterly Life Design Plan'.

There are three parts to your Quarterly Life Design Plan:

1. Choosing what you want the next three months to be all about

This is where you set the tone for the next quarter and decide what you want it to be all about. You might decide to focus on your intention for the year, on a particular project or simply on feeling a certain way.

2. Writing down the activities, experiences, people, places, trips and projects you want you life to be full of over the next three months

This is where you get to write down all the ingredients you'd love your life to be full of over the next three months. Never put anything on this list that you think you should be doing. Only write down the things you really want to have filling up your life.

3. Committing to doing three things over the next three months that have you living a life you love

Choose three things that you most want to focus on and commit to over the next three months. For each commitment choose either a specific goal that you can schedule into your calendar, a habit that you want to form in your life (again, which you can schedule into your calendar) or an intention that you want to anchor yourself to.

MY QUARTERLY LIFE DESIGN PLAN
1ST JANUARY - 31ST MARCH

What I'm going to focus on creating, cultivating and making happen in my life over the next three months:

What do you want these next three months to be all about?

What activities, experiences, people, places, trips and projects do you want your life to be filled with over the next three months?

What three things do you commit to focusing on, doing or making happen over the next 3 months?

1.

2.

3.

SCHEDULE IT INTO YOUR CALENDAR

YOUR CALENDAR IS YOUR CANVAS

When it comes to designing a life you love, your calendar is your canvas. It is the magic wand that helps to take your dreams and intentions off the page and into your life, until you are living them.

So, if you don't use a calendar or you have a calendar, but only use it for work, doctors appointments and social arrangements, then you're about to discover the true power a calendar can have to design your life and make your dreams come true.

How to use a calendar to design a life you love

1. Choose a calendar with hourly slots

Whether you choose a digital or a paper calendar, what you need is a calendar that has hourly slots in it and where you can see the whole week laid out in front of you.

If you don't yet have a calendar like that, then make it a top priority to get yourself one this week!

2. Use your calendar to schedule the things you want to fill your life with, including the three commitments from your Quarterly Life Design Plan

To do that, you need to get specific with your commitments, so if one of your commitments is, for example, 'learn to cook', you'll need to get specific about how, where, when and how often. For example, you might decide 'I'm going to learn to cook one new dish every Wednesday night'.

There might also then be some other steps you need to schedule into your calendar, such as 'time to gather a list of online recipes or buy a new recipe book'.

Once you're clear on the steps you need to take, open up your calendar and schedule them all in!

"Your inner knowing is your only true compass."

Joy Page

INNER

GUIDE

SAY HELLO TO YOUR INNER WISE CHEERLEADER

Now you've set your intention for 2026, got clear on the dreams you want to go after and have a plan of how you're going to make it all happen, there is one final step you need to take to really get this journey started:

It's time to say hello to your Inner Wise Cheerleader.

We often think that the support, guidance and encouragement we need can only come from other people, but actually you have the power to give yourself the guidance and encouragement you most need as you set out to go after your dreams.

All you have to do is imagine that a wise and supportive person is writing you a message of encouragement as you embark on going after your dreams in 2026. And on the following page, write that message to yourself.

If you've never done this kind of thing before, it might sound a little crazy, but as soon as you give it a go and just start writing, you'll be amazed at just how much support and wisdom can emerge on the page in front of you.

A message from my Inner Wise Cheerleader:

"Be sure that what you are doing is moving you toward where you want to go."

– Ruben Chavez

RTERLY
CK-INS

QUARTERLY CHECK-INS

Now that you have filled in this journal with your intention, dreams and desires for 2026, it will act as a guide and toolkit to support you as you design a life you love throughout the year, helping to remind you of the life you want to be living, the ingredients you need to feel truly happy and fulfilled and the dreams you want to make happen.

Come back to reconnect with your intentions and your dreams on pages 47 to 58 whenever you need to.

And at the start of April, July and October return to this section to do your quarterly check-in. You'll be guided through a series of questions that will help you reflect on the three months you've just lived through and make a fresh **Quarterly Life Design Plan** for the next three months to come.

GET A REMINDER WHEN IT IS TIME FOR YOUR QUARTERLY CHECK-INS

Sign up to the Goodbye Hello Club (it's free!) and get a reminder every quarter when it is time to do your quarterly check-in! Plus you can join live journaling sessions where you can fill in your journal with Goodbye, Hello fans all over the world!

Join the club today by scanning the QR code below or going to projectyoujournals.com/ goodbye-hello-club

YOUR LiFe IS
ONE BIG CANVAS.
AND YOU ARE
THE ARTIST.
PAINT IT WiTH THE
THINGS YOU LOVE.

– Selina Barker

APRIL

APRIL REFLECTIONS

It's time to take a step back and reflect on the past three months –
on all that you've done, the lessons you've learnt, your happiest
moments, the challenges you've faced and overcome...

How are you feeling at the moment?

What has happened in your life since January?

What have been your happiest moments?

What have been your most challenging moments?

What are you proud of yourself for?

What and who do you feel grateful for at this moment in your life?

Read back through the dreams and desires that you wrote down in pages 25 to 73 and write down the ones that became a reality this quarter:

How did you get on with your three quarterly commitments and what did you learn from doing (or not doing) them?

MY QUARTERLY LIFE DESIGN PLAN
1ST APRIL - 30TH JUNE

What do you want these next three months to be all about?

What activities, experiences, people, places, trips and projects do you want your life to be filled with over the next three months?

What three things do you commit to focusing on, doing or making happen over the next 3 months?

1.

2.

3.

Now go and schedule your three commitments into your calendar!

DON'T GET SO BUSY MAKING A LIVING THAT YOU FORGET TO MAKE A LIFE.

– Dolly Parton

JULY

JULY REFLECTIONS

It's time to take a step back and reflect on the past three months – on all that you've done, the lessons you've learnt, your happiest moments, the challenges you've faced and overcome...

How are you feeling at the moment?

What has happened in your life since April?

What have been your happiest moments?

What have been your most challenging moments?

What are you proud of yourself for?

What and who do you feel grateful for at this moment in your life?

Read back through the dreams and desires that you wrote down in pages 25 to 82 and write down the ones that became a reality this quarter:

How did you get on with your three quarterly commitments and what did you learn from doing (or not doing) them?

MY QUARTERLY LIFE DESIGN PLAN
1ST JULY - 30TH SEPTEMBER

What do you want these next three months to be all about?

What activities, experiences, people, places, trips and projects do you want your life to be filled with over the next three months?

What three things do you commit to focusing on, doing or making happen over the next 3 months?

1.

2.

3.

Now go and schedule your three commitments into your calendar!

YOUR TIME IS LIMITED, SO DON'T WASTE IT LIVING SOMEONE ELSE'S LIFE.

– Steve Jobs

OCTOBER

OCToBER REFLECTiONS

It's time to take a step back and reflect on the past three months – on all that you've done, the lessons you've learnt, your happiest moments, the challenges you've faced and overcome...

How are you feeling at the moment?

What has happened in your life since July?

What have been your happiest moments?

What have been your most challenging moments?

What are you proud of yourself for?

What and who do you feel grateful for at this moment in your life?

Read back through the dreams and desires that you wrote down in pages 25 to 88 and write down the ones that became a reality this quarter:

How did you get on with your three quarterly commitments and what did you learn from doing (or not doing) them?

MY QUARTERLY LIFE DESIGN PLAN
1ST OCTOBER - 31ST DECEMBER

What do you want these next three months to be all about?

What activities, experiences, people, places, trips and projects do you want your life to be filled with over the next three months?

What three things do you commit to focusing on, doing or making happen over the next 3 months?

1.

2.

3.

Now go and schedule your three commitments into your calendar!

YOUR DREAMS ARE WAITING. IT'S NOT TOO LATE — YOU'RE RIGHT ON TIME.

–Unknown

"The past is not just something to leave behind. It's something to learn from, to honour, and to grow beyond."

– Maya Angelou

TIME TO RE

FLECT

A FINAL REFLECTION

And so we've come to the end of another year. It is time to take a step back and reflect on all that has happened in 2026 and, in particular, on which of the intentions and dreams, written into the pages of this journal, have become a reality in your life this past year.

Now, not all of those intentions and dreams will have materialised and that's ok. Some dream seeds grow and flourish and others don't.

For now, it's time to reflect on the dreams that you wrote down in this journal that did come true and how setting an intention for your year helped guide your choices and shape your life.

So let's start by taking a look at your intention for 2026.

2026 was my year of:

What has it been like to have this as your focus for a year?

How did you help to make your 2026 about that?

Read back through the dreams and desires that you wrote down in pages 47 to 94 and write down the ones that did happen:

Is there anything you wrote down that didn't happen this year and you wish it had?

What can you do to help make that happen in 2027?

As you look back on 2026 and the dreams you brought to life and the intentions that shaped your year, take a moment to celebrate yourself. Celebrate your power to create your own reality and your ability to bring your dreams to life and to materialise the changes you wanted to see in your own life and the world around you.

How does it feel to know that you can be the artist of your own life and are taking steps, big and small, to create the life you want to be living?

AND SUDDENLY YOU KNOW: IT'S TIME TO START SOMETHING NEW WTHE MAGIC OF BEGINNINGS.

– Meister Eckhart

GOODBYE FoR NOW

And so with that, your **Goodbye 2025, Hello 2026** journey is complete! Forgive yourself if there were any dreams, intentions or commitments that you didn't bring to life this year. It's not about getting a perfect score (not at all!). Instead, focus on what you **did** create and make happen in your life. And celebrate!

Life design, at its core, is about recognising that you have the power to be the artist of your own life. You possess the magic that all human beings have, of being able to make your dreams a reality.

All it takes is the willingness to allow yourself to dream, take those dreams seriously and turn them into projects and actions that, step by step, will bring those dreams to life.

So grab a hold of that magic that you possess and we'll see you over in the **Goodbye 2026, Hello 2027** journal for another year of creating a life you love!

With all our love,

x Selina

Order your copy of the Goodbye 2026, Hello 2027 journal over at
projectyoujournals.com

NOTES

NOTES

NOTES

NOTES

NOTES

NOTES

NOTES

LOVE AND THANKS

With special thanks to Lou Desborough for designing this beauty, the KOPA team in Lithuania for taking such great care over printing it, the shops that have stocked it, every single person that has told their friends and followers about it (thank you!) and the Project You community for being such a constant source of love, support and inspiration - this journal is for you ♡

First published in the United Kingdom in 2025 by Project You
Copyright © Selina Barker Ltd 2025
Text copyright © Selina Barker Ltd 2025

All rights reserved. No part of this publication may be copied, displayed,
extracted, reproduced, utilized, stored in a retrieval system or transmitted in
any form or by any means, electronic, mechanical or otherwise including but
not limited to photocopying, recording or scanning without the prior written
permission of the publishers.

ISBN: 978-1-0687258-1-4

Printed and bound by KOPA, Lithuania

projectyoujournals.com @projectyoujournals